CREATIVE CRAFTS for CRITTERS

Nancy Furstinger
Philippe Beha

Stoddart
Kids
TORONTO • NEW YORK

*Dedicated to that heavenly masterpiece — the dog —
especially Pretzel, Jazmine, Ariel, and Sasha Starfoot,
who left their pawprints on my heart.
And to Diamond Dreamer, my wizard of mirth.*
—N.F.

Text copyright © 2000 by Nancy Furstinger
Illustrations copyright © 2000 by Philippe Beha

Published in Canada in 2000 by
Stoddart Kids,
a division of Stoddart Publishing Co. Limited
34 Lesmill Road
Toronto, ON M3B 2T6
Tel (416) 445-3333 Fax (416) 445-5967
E-mail cservice@genpub.com

Distributed in Canada by
General Distribution Services
325 Humber College Blvd.,
Toronto, ON M9W 7C3
Tel (416) 213-1919 Fax (416) 213-1917
E-mail cservice@genpub.com

Published in the United States in 2001 by
Stoddart Kids,
a division of Stoddart Publishing Co. Limited
180 Varick Street, 9th Floor
New York, New York 10014
Toll free 1-800-805-1083
E-mail gdsinc@genpub.com

Distributed in the United States by
General Distribution Services
4500 Witmer Industrial Estates, PMB 128
Niagara Falls, New York 14305-1386
Toll free 1-800-805-1083
E-mail gdsinc@genpub.com

Canadian Cataloguing in Publication Data

Furstinger, Nancy
Creative crafts for critters

ISBN 0-7737-6135-7

1. Handicraft – Juvenile literature. 2. Pet supplies – Juvenile literature.
3. Pets – Feeding and feeds – Recipes – Juvenile literature.
I. Beha, Philippe. II. Title.

TT160.F87 2000   j745.5   C00-931092-4

Easy-to-make crafts, projects, and health care tips for common household pets.

THE CANADA COUNCIL   LE CONSEIL DES ARTS
FOR THE ARTS   DU CANADA
SINCE 1957   DEPUIS 1957

*We acknowledge for their financial support of our
publishing program the Canada Council, the Ontario Arts
Council, and the Government of Canada through the
Book Publishing Industry Development Program (BPIDP).*

Printed and bound in Hong Kong, China
by Book Art Inc., Toronto

Contents

Catnip Container Garden

Cats go crazy for catnip. It captivates most kitties from about seven months of age. They love to nibble and roll around in this delicious, minty herb. Here's how to grow a catnip garden for your special cat.

Materials

pencil	bottom third of a milk carton
saucer	equal parts peat and sand
catnip seeds	clear plastic bag
scissors	string
brown paper bag	

Instructions

1. Use the pencil point to punch small holes in the bottom of the milk carton. Place it on a saucer.

2. Fill the carton to the top with the peat/sand mixture. Plant the catnip seeds about 1 cm (1/2 inch) deep. Water well.

3. Cover with a clear plastic bag. Put the container in a sunny spot. Keep the soil moist. Protect the seedlings from your curious cat.

4. When the plants have grown about the height of your little finger, take off the plastic, and give the container to your pet to enjoy. Or, you can break off a fresh leaf and watch your cat turn into a clown.

5. Or, hide the catnip from kitty until you can harvest it. Snip the catnip stems when the flower buds open. Tie string around bunches of the stems. Hang the stems upside down in a dark closet. The catnip should be dry in about a week. Gently crumble the dried leaves and stems. Save the dried catnip in a brown paper bag. Give your kitty a little pinch of it once in a while, and watch her have a ball! Or make the Teddy Toy on page 6.

Tabby's Teddy Toy

Forget mice! What your kitty really craves is a teddy to call his own. He'll be purring with joy after you create this catnip-filled toy. It's easy to make, and you can fill it with home-grown or store-bought catnip.

Materials

tracing paper	pencil
cotton fabric	pins
needle	thread
scissors	fiberfill stuffing
dried catnip	non-toxic permanent markers

Instructions

1. Trace the teddy pattern onto tracing paper. (The pattern should be enlarged on a photocopier.) Cut out the pattern.

2. Fold your fabric in half so the good sides face in.

3. Pin the pattern to the fabric.

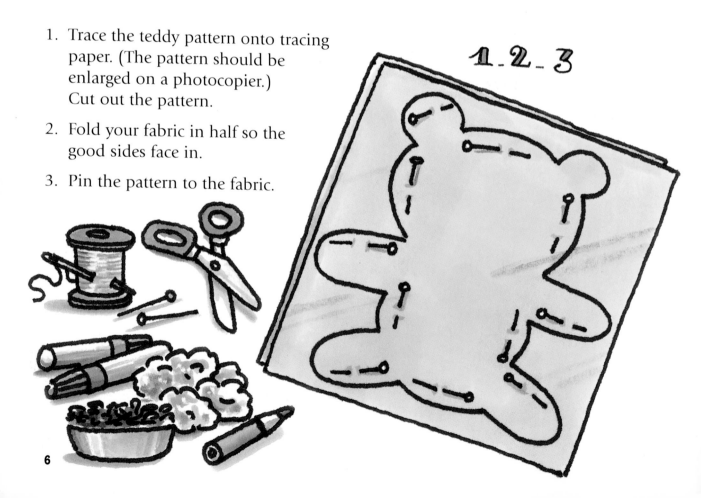

4. Cut around the pattern through both pieces of fabric. Remove the pattern and re-pin the fabric together.

5. Thread your needle. Knot the end of the thread.

6. Use a running stitch. Stitch 6 mm (1/4 inch) in from the edge. Each stitch should be about 3 mm (1/8 inch) long. Keeping the thread pulled firmly, make neat, even stitches.

7. Leave the space between the two ears open. Make an ending knot by sewing several stitches, one on top of the other. Leave the thread loose, so it forms a loop. Weave the needle and thread through this loop. Pull tight. Snip off any extra thread. Remove all pins.

8. Turn your teddy bear right side out.

9. Poke a combination of catnip and stuffing into the gap. Don't overfill.

10. Pin the gap closed. Sew along the gap, using tiny stitches. Make an ending knot.

11. With the markers, draw a face on the teddy bear.

12. Pinch the teddy bear to release the scented oils in the catnip.

Personalized Pet Collar

What a fun way to show off your creativity! Why not decorate several of these collars for the best-dressed pet in your neighborhood?

Materials

cardboard	nylon pet collar*
soft pencil	bottles of squeeze-on fabric
paper towels	paint

* For correct collar size, measure around your pet's neck. Then add 5 cm (2 inches) to the measurement.

Instructions

1. With the squeeze-on fabric paint, practice making the following designs on a piece of cardboard:

   To make beads, squeeze and lift the paint tip.

   For box letters, script, and squiggles: squeeze at a steady pace. Squeeze quickly for fine lines; squeeze slowly for thick lines.

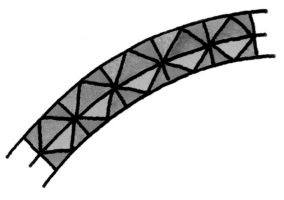

2. Once you've become an expert, it's time to decorate. Place the collar flat and right side up. Use a soft pencil to outline your design on the collar. Now choose your first color of fabric paint. Keep your hand steady. If a break in your painted design occurs, go back and fill it in. Use paper towels to keep the paint tips clean.

3. After you've finished your design, let it dry for three days.

Hints

Try shiny black to write your pet's name or initial. Decorate with colors for added pizzazz. Draw a profile (side view) of your pet's head. Add colorful touches: flowers, rainbows, butterflies, stars, and moons. If you're feeling very van Gogh, decorate a nylon leash to match!

Cat Attack!!!

Watch your cat go bonkers as she gets an aerobic workout!

Materials

five fun objects to mix or match: pompoms, small bells, fish-shaped felt cut-outs, feathers, crumpled paper, bows, big buttons, spools

cotton work glove (from garden or hardware store)
embroidery floss
embroidery needle

Instructions

1. Thread the needle with a length of embroidery floss. Tie a double knot at one end of the floss.

2. Pull the needle with floss through the first fingertip of the glove. Remove the needle.

3. Tie the other end of the floss securely around a fun object. Repeat for each finger.

4. Put the glove on. Call your cat over. Wiggle your fingers and let the fun begin.

(Note: This is a craft to share with your cat. Don't let her play with it alone.)

Treasure Box

Do you need a place to store your critter's stuff? Treats, toys, combs, and brushes — they all can be stashed in this fun-to-make box. Decorate with cutouts or photos to invent a nifty, one-of-a-kind masterpiece.

Materials

pictures	scissors
glue	newspaper
shoebox	paintbrush
clear lacquer	

Instructions

1. Collect pictures. Try searching through pet care catalogues, your own photos, magazines, and old postcards and greeting cards.

2. Cut out the pictures. Be creative! Experiment with different artistic designs.

3. Once you are happy with your arrangement, begin gluing. Protect your work surface with newspaper. Cover all four sides and the top lid of the shoebox with pictures.

4. Give the glue time to dry. Then, protect your découpage box by painting it with a thin coat of lacquer. If you want a super shine, add another coat after the first one has dried. Your beautiful box is ready to be filled!

Biscuit Frame

This colorful frame is perfect for displaying the smile on your furry pal's face. Use green and red biscuits to make a cool Christmas present for your aunt's angora or your best friend's beagle.

Materials

newspaper	4 strips of cardboard, 15 cm
8 colored dog biscuits,	(6 inches) x 2.5 cm (1 inch)
5.7 cm (2.25 inches) long	4 colored dog biscuits, 2.5 cm
clear gloss polyurethane	(1 inch) long
glue gel	foam poly-brush
hole puncher	cardboard square, 15 cm x 15 cm
cord, 61cm (2 feet)	(6 inch x 6 inch)

Instructions

1. Cover your work surface with newspaper. Brush the top and sides of all 12 biscuits with polyurethane. Let them dry for 24 hours.

2. Glue the strips of cardboard together, overlapping the top and bottom strips, to form a square.

3. When dry, glue 2 of the larger biscuits on each side of the frame. Let the glue dry. Then glue 1 smaller biscuit at each corner, on top of the bigger biscuits. Let the frame dry overnight.

4. Make a hole in the top center of the cardboard square. Loop the cord through the hole. Tie a double knot.

5. Glue the biscuit frame to the cardboard square along the top and both sides. Leave the bottom open. Allow the glue to dry.

6. Slip in the pet's photo. Hang it where all can admire.

Massage Mitt

Your cat or dog will beg for a massage session as soon as you slip on this terry mitt.

Materials

terry washcloth	pins
needle	thread
scissors	large sewing snap

Instructions

1. Place your hand (right or left) on the top of half of the washcloth. Fold the other half over, covering your hand.

2. Have an adult loosely pin around your hand. It will be shaped like a big mitten. Carefully remove your hand from the mitt.

3. Thread the needle and knot the end of the thread.

4. Use a running stitch. Stitch along the pin line. Leave the bottom open so your hand can get in. Each stitch should be about 3 mm (1/8 inch) long. Keeping the thread pulled firmly, make neat, even stitches.

5. End by sewing three stitches, one on top of the other. Leave the thread loose on the last one, so it forms a loop. Weave the needle

and thread through this loop. Pull tight. Snip off extra thread. Remove all pins.

6. Cut around the side and top, about 2.5 cm (1 inch) out from the sewing line. Turn the mitt right side out.

7. Sew the snap and fastener at the bottom of the mitt. Position them so the mitt will fit snugly on your hand.

8. Put on your mitt and begin the Magical Pet Massage. (see next page)

Magical Pet Massage

Most animals adore a relaxing massage. This is a wonderful gift for your favorite buddy and, best of all, it's free!

Instructions

1. Catch your pet in a relaxed mood. Have her stretch out on a towel.

2. Start by gently stroking, from the head toward the tail, with your mitt on.

3. You might sprinkle a few drops of massage oil (use sparingly — recipe follows) on your mitt.

4. Once you're sure your pal is enjoying this, try a massage stroke. Remove the mitt. Place both hands on either side of her spine. Circle your thumbs inward, toward your fingers. Use light pressure. Slowly work your way down her spine and back up again.

5. Finish by slipping on the mitt and repeating step two. Your pet will be on cloud canine.

Pet Perfume

Use this spicy, scented massage oil to give your pet's coat a glossy shine.

Instructions

- To 125 mL (1/2 cup) olive oil, add 2 mL (1/2 teaspoon) of each of the following:

- Ground allspice, ground cinnamon, and pure vanilla extract. Stir until blended and let stand overnight. Filter by pouring through a paper towel into a clean jar. Cover tightly.

Hair Flare

You can create these nifty hair ornaments in a jiffy. (If your canine or feline has short hair, these make cool collar decorations.)

Materials

ribbons	latex dog grooming bands
glue	lace
sequins	pompons
beads	silk flowers
charms	barrettes
paintbrush	enamel paints

Instructions

Bows:

Invade your sewing basket or purchase ribbon from a craft shop. At the center of a length of ribbon loop one end of a latex band through the other and pull. Tie a simple bow with the ribbon. Add the final touch with a dot of glue and a decoration.

Barrettes:

Personalize plain barrettes by painting miniature designs on them. Try pawprints, your dog or cat's name, a mouse, or bones. Or use glue to cover the barrettes with decorations.

Hints

Go for the gusto with larger breeds. Giant bows and ponytail-sized barrettes in bright colors won't get lost in fur. Special events call for elegant fabrics. Try black velvet bows with a center of white lace. Silk daisies on green satin bows are nice for spring. A barrette covered with pearl beads adds a well-bred touch. But remember! Never leave bows or barrettes on your pet when you aren't around. They are for wearing, not for chewing!

Pet Portfolio

Pedigreed or not, your faithful friend needs to keep her photos, certificates, and other papers from becoming dog-eared. This portfolio will organize health records, obedience class diplomas, and special memories of your friendship.

Materials

2 pieces of cardboard, 21.6 x 28 cm (8-1/2 x 11 inches)	sheets of construction paper, 21.6 x 28 cm (8-1/2 x 11 inches)
hole puncher	yarn and ribbon
scissors	glue stick
stamp pad	photo corners
colored pens	

Instructions

1. Glue a sheet of construction paper to each piece of cardboard. This will be your portfolio cover.

2. Decorate the cover of your portfolio. Carefully print your pet's name and birthdate. Underneath, use a stamp pad to print one of your pet's pawprints. Have an adult snip off a length of fur or save a feather that has fallen out. Then you can tie it with a ribbon and glue it on the cover.

3. Add a baby picture of your best friend. Trace the outline of your photo on a sheet of construction paper. Pick a color that is different from the cover. Cut a window inside the outline you drew. Then cut a frame around the window for your photo. Glue the picture and frame to the portfolio cover.

4. Sandwich sheets of construction paper between the covers. Punch a hole at the top and the bottom left corners.

5. Loop yarn through the two holes. Tie it in the front with a big bow.

6. Create folders to hold important documents. Glue two pieces of hole-punched construction paper together around the sides and bottom edges. Leave the top open. Make a label by cutting a pawprint shape out of construction paper. On it, write a description of papers stashed in the folder.

7. Add photos of special moments. Mount them on construction paper using four photo corners. Write captions underneath.

Pet Place Mat

Keep doggy drool and cat crumbs off the floor with this fetching place mat.

Materials

magic marker	pinking shears
piece of cloth, 43 cm x 28 cm (17 inch x 11 inch)	clear contact paper twice the length of your cloth
alphabet stencils (optional)	fabric paints
paintbrushes	*scissors and/or x-acto knife

Instructions

1. Trim cloth edges with pinking shears for a decorative edge. This also prevents material from fraying.

2. Cut the contact paper in half so that you have two pieces the size of your cloth. Set one aside. Sketch a stencil design on the contact paper. Try hearts, mice, or bones. Cut the stencil pattern out of the paper. *Ask an adult for help

3. Now transfer your design to the cloth. Peel off the backing and place the contact paper sticky side down onto the material. With a circular motion, brush paint over the stencil. Use a clean paintbrush for each color. You might decide on an all-over pattern, a border, your pet's name, or a stencil in each corner.

4. Let it dry overnight. Carefully remove the contact paper.

5. Protect and waterproof your place mat. Stick the second sheet of clear contact paper over the cloth and press down firmly.

Hints

With alphabet stencils, you can write your pet's name or a phrase. How about MOUSEBREATH DINER or CHOW HOUND DELI?

Easy Cheesy Treats

Reward your favorite dog or cat with these all-natural treats. Even finicky felines and gourmutt canines give this recipe a four-paw rating.

Ingredients and tools

1 egg
75 mL (1/3 cup) olive oil
50 mL (1/4 cup) chopped, fresh parsley
measuring cups and spoons
mixing spoon
waxed paper
non-stick cookie sheet
spatula

30 mL (2 tablespoons) buttermilk
125 mL (1/2 cup) grated cheddar cheese
2 cloves minced garlic
250 mL (1 cup) stone-ground whole wheat flour
large bowl
sifter
plastic knife

Instructions

1. Beat the egg and buttermilk together in the bowl.

2. Slowly mix in the oil, cheese, parsley, and garlic.

3. Keep stirring as you sift in the flour. The dough will be stiff.

4. Dump the dough on a sheet of waxed paper. Use your hands to roll it into a long snake.

5. Roll up the dough in the waxed paper. Freeze it for two hours until firm.

6. Cut 2.5 cm (1 inch) slices from the dough snake. Place them onto a cookie sheet. Then, have an adult help you bake the treats at 180°C (350°F) for about 15 minutes until brown.

7. Lift the treats off the cookie sheet with a spatula. Let them cool for 15 minutes. Serve one or two with a bowl of fresh water and store the rest for another day. Paws-itively delicious!

Party Animal Snacks

Celebrate Bowser's bash or Mitten's mixer in style. Your pet's guests will drool when these tasty pup pies and cat cakes are served. No doggie bags required — there won't be any leftovers!

Ingredients and tools

250 mL (1 cup) cottage cheese
125 mL (1/2 cup) milk
250 mL (1 cup) grated
   cheddar cheese
mixing spoon
tablespoon

500 mL (2 cups) combination
   of chopped tomatoes and
   zucchini
3 eggs
mixing bowl
two nonstick muffin tins or
   small cake pans
candles

Instructions

1. Mix the cottage cheese, vegetables, milk, grated cheese, and eggs together in a bowl.

2. Use the mixing spoon to distribute the mixture evenly into the tins.

3. With an adult's help, bake at 180°C (350°F) for about 30 minutes. The snacks should be firm.

4. Let them cool for 10 minutes. To remove, slide the mixing spoon handle around the edges of the quiches. Turn them upside down onto a plate.

5. For a birthday treat, place a candle in the center of each snack. Have an adult light the candles. Sing a chorus of Happy Birthday. Blow out the candles for your pet.

Makes 12 tail-wagging, whisker-licking servings. Bone appetite!

Flying Fruit Cup

This fun food toy is for the birds. They'll nibble on the tasty treats and play with the orange cup.

Materials

large orange	plastic knife
serrated citrus spoon	pencil
3 leather bootlaces	small metal clip like the fastener at the end of a dog leash (from the hardware store)

Some treats to try: shelled peanuts, apple wedges, whole strawberries, grapes, cranberries, kiwi, sliced banana, coconut, pineapple, dried fruits, raisins, dates, sunflower seeds, carrots, romaine lettuce, green beans, zucchini, popcorn, cereal, unsalted pretzels

Instructions

1. Cut the orange in half with the knife. Use the spoon to scoop out the fruit from the rind.

2. With the pencil, carefully punch three evenly spaced holes through the rind, about 2.5 cm (1 inch) from the cut end.

3. Knot one end of each bootlace and thread through the holes. Tie the ends of the laces to the metal clip. Hang the fruit cup from the top of the birdcage.

4. Fill with an assortment of treats. Replace with fresh treats each day.

Surprise Nibble Box

Your feathered friend will enjoy nibbling the snack and shredding the box.

Materials

snack-sized box from raisins or cereal	raisins, cereal, peanuts, popcorn

Instructions

1. Stuff the box with snacks.
2. Close the box back up.
3. Stand back and watch the fun begin!

Sunshine Sprouts

Your canary will cartwheel and your budgie will backflip when you serve crunchy sprouts. These living vegetables are delicious and nutritious. And they're super-fresh because you grow them right in your kitchen.

Materials

large glass jar with lid	scissors
magic marker	mesh (cheesecloth or old
rubber band	nylon stocking)
oat groats	tablespoon

Instructions

1. Pour 30 mL (2 tablespoons) of oat groats into the jar. Make sure the groats are fresh or they won't sprout. Add enough warm water to completely cover the groats.

2. Place the jar lid on top of the cheesecloth or stocking. Trace around it with a magic marker. Now draw a second, bigger circle around the first. Using the second circle as your guide, cut the mesh.

3. Fasten the mesh over the jar, with the rubber band to hold it in place.

4. Put the jar in a sunny, warm spot in your kitchen. Allow the groats to soak for 24 hours.

5. Pour out the excess water through the mesh. Rinse the groats with warm water and drain well.

6. Twice a day, rinse and drain the sprouts.

7. In about a week, you'll have oat groat sprouts. Give your bird a serving of these crunchy greens. Store the leftovers in the refrigerator. Rinse with cold water to keep the sprouts crisp. You can also try sprouting a variety of fresh grains: millet, hemp, even your bird's seed.

Goldfish Garden

Grow a garden of earthworms for your goldfish to snack on. They're easy to raise and tasty for your fishy friend.

Materials

cardboard shoebox with
  holes poked in lid
foil drip pan
watering can
cornmeal
old tablespoon

waxed paper
peat moss (from garden store)
6 wooden blocks
box of small earthworms (from
  bait store)

Instructions

1. Line the shoebox with waxed paper. Fill the box with peat moss. Put the box into the foil drip pan.

2. Place one block underneath each front corner of the shoebox. Place two blocks underneath each back corner. The shoebox will be on a slant.

3. Use the watering can to soak the peat moss.

4. Now put the worms in the box. Sprinkle the peat moss lightly with about a tablespoon (15 mL) of cornmeal. Earthworms like it dark so put the lid on the box.

5. Find a good spot for your earthworm garden, such as a garage, closet, or kitchen cabinet. Don't allow the worms to freeze or get baked by the sun.

6. Every three days, gently stir up the peat moss with the old tablespoon. Then add another spoonful of cornmeal.

7. Keep the peat moss damp by watering once a week.

8. In about a month, you'll have a worm nursery. Feed the baby worms to your goldfish. Yummy — wiggly spaghetti!

Earthworms also make a healthy treat for your garden.

Abracadabra Budgie Chains

Treats will vanish from these chains like magic! When the goodies are gone, your bird can play with the beads and bell.

Materials

piece of twine, twice as long as cage height	scissors
uncooked tube pasta, small unsalted pretzels, cereal with holes in the middle	4 large-sized beads or buttons
	bell with large clapper

Instructions

1. Tie a knot 10 cm (4 inches) in from one end of the twine. Make sure the knot is big enough so the beads or buttons cannot slip off.

2. Slip a bead or button on. Tie another knot about 2.5 cm (1 inch) from the first knot.

3. Then slip on a piece of pasta, a pretzel, and several pieces of cereal. Tie a knot close to the strand of food.

4. Repeat steps 2 and 3.

5. Tie the bell onto the twine. This will be the middle of the chain.

6. Repeat steps 3 and 2 twice.

7. Make a circle out of the chain by tying both ends of the twine to the top of the birdcage. Cut off the excess twine.

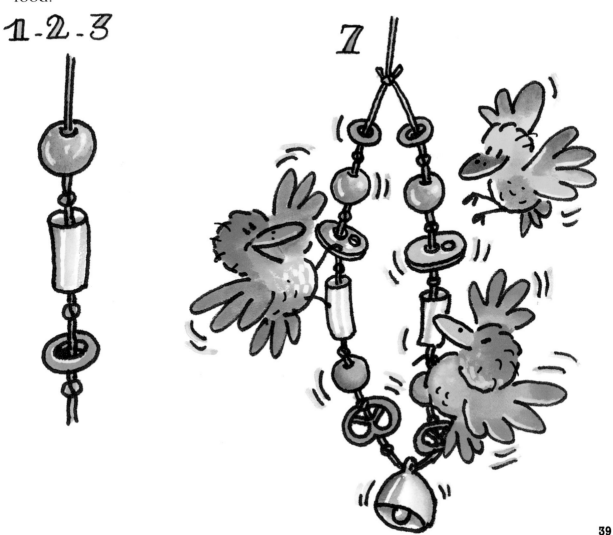

Tantalizing Tightrope

This toy is great for your feathered friend's aerobic workout. Birds have sharp vision and can see colors, so use bright ones to entertain them.

Materials

3 long strips of leather	wooden clothespins
pipecleaners	Popsicle sticks
vegetable food coloring	paper cups
2 hanging toys, such as plastic rings or rattles	crackers and pretzels
	small eyebolt

Instructions

1. Loosely braid the strips of leather together. This will form the tightrope.

2. Wrap some pipe cleaners around a section of the tightrope.

3. Slip one hanging toy onto the tightrope.

4. Dye the Popsicle sticks. Fill paper cups with water. Add several drops of food coloring to each cup. Soak the sticks for about 15 minutes, until they are brightly colored. Let the sticks dry.

5. Insert the sticks through loops in the braid.

6. Repeat steps 2 and 3.

7. Tie one end of the tightrope to the cage and the other end to a small eyebolt. Ask an adult to fasten the eyebolt to a wall or secure object.

8. Use the clothespins to clip on treats such as crackers and unsalted pretzels.

Pocket-Pet Palace

Do you have a pocket-pet such as a rabbit, guinea pig, hamster, gerbil, mouse, or rat? Your small animal will have fun exploring his new playhouse. As a bonus, your pocket-pet will be keeping both his body and brain busy.

Materials

2 cardboard boxes (one about the size of your pet, the other twice as large)	scissors
	pieces of cardboard or squashed boxes
cardboard tubes from paper towel and toilet paper rolls, oatmeal containers with bottoms removed, or clothes dryer exhaust tubing (for a small pet)	cardboard concrete forms (sono-tubes) — available from home building supply stores
	masking tape
	unscented paper towels
	wooden block
long, narrow cardboard boxes the size of your pet with ends removed (for a large pet)	non-toxic permanent markers
	piece of plywood (about three times the height of your pet)
rug scrap or old towel	

Instructions

1. Start with the smaller cardboard box. Remove one end so your pet can crawl inside.

2. Put several pieces of cardboard or squashed boxes on the floor. Place the smaller box on top of this.

3. Place the larger box over the smaller one, upside down, so that the open side faces the floor. Cut out door holes on three sides of the box. These should be a little larger than your pet.

4. Decorate the box with your markers. Draw a picture of your pet and a fancy plaque with his or her name.

5. Grasping a paper towel, pull a 2.5 cm. (1 inch) strip all the way down. Keep ripping shreds until you have a pile of burrowing material. Stuff handfuls of the shredded paper towels inside the large box.

6. Now invent a maze for your pet using the tubes, containers, exhaust tubing, cardboard concrete forms, or cardboard boxes. You can join them by cutting doorways and using masking tape on the outside to stick them together. Make sure your pet can run through them without getting stuck.

7. Create a ramp by propping the piece of plywood up on the wooden block. Cover the ramp with the rug or wrap it with the towel. Place the ramp so it leads up to the top of the large box. Your pet will be on top of the world!

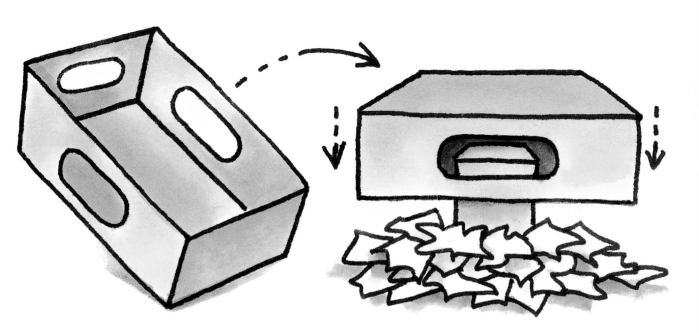

Note:

Be sure to supervise your pet during the play session as this is NOT a caged activity. Smaller animals can easily scurry out of sight if not watched carefully.

Pocket-Pet Playground

Here's a great playground to watch your pocket-pet play, snack, and nap in. It's portable, so you can set up this pet daycare center anywhere. It includes three fun toys to toss and munch on!

Materials

litterbox or dishpan
cardboard tube from paper
  towel or toilet paper roll
small bowl
hard plastic caps from laundry
  softener bottles

fresh hay (timothy, oat, or alfalfa)
pinecone
honey in plastic squeeze bottle
raw peanuts, rolled oats, wheat germ
natural wicker wastebasket or large
  paper sack

Instructions

1. Fill the litterbox or dishpan with fresh hay.

2. Stuff the cardboard tube with hay. Make sure hay sticks out at both ends. This makes a terrific toss-and-chew toy.

3. Wash and dry the pinecone. Squeeze on a few drops of honey. Mix together the raw peanuts, rolled oats, and wheat germ in a small bowl. Roll the pinecone around in this mixture until it's covered. It makes a dandy treat for snack time.

4. Put the pinecone and tube toy in the litterbox or dishpan.

5. Wash the plastic caps thoroughly. Stack them up in a tall column next to the litterbox or dishpan. Your pet will have a great time knocking them down.

6. Lay the wastebasket or sack on its side. Stick one corner of the litterbox or dishpan inside the wastebasket or sack to hold it down. This makes a nifty hideaway cave.

7. Add your pet and watch the games begin!

Pet Care Tips

- Have your male pet neutered and your female pet spayed. There are not enough homes for the many litters of animals born each day.

- Take him to the veterinarian once a year for a checkup and vaccinations.

- Always have fresh, clean water nearby for your pet. Make sure the water doesn't freeze in the winter or evaporate in the summer. Clean the bowl or bottle daily.

- Groom your pal's coat regularly. Have an adult help you clean her ears and trim her nails. Clean, healthy pets are less likely to attract fleas and parasites.

- Exercise is important and can be fun for pets. Grab a leash and take your dog for a walk. Dangle the Cat Attack!!! in front of your couch-potato kitty. Watch your bird as he balances on the Tantalizing Tightrope. Play a game of stack-up caps with your hamster.

- Feed your pet a healthy diet. Ask your vet's advice. Reward your best pal with homemade treats from this book. But remember, snacks should not make up more than ten percent of your pet's diet.

- Teach your pet good manners. Take your dog to obedience classes or train him yourself. (There are books available on the subject.) Never hit your pet — use a blend of patience and praise.

- Keep your pet's zone clean. Scoop up poop. Wash bowls and beds thoroughly. Empty and disinfect your cat or rabbit's litterbox. Your bird or pocket-pet's cage should be scrubbed weekly. Clean your fish's tank regularly.

- Pet-proof your home. Remove all unsafe items within reach, such as plants, candles, toys, sharp objects, chemicals, medicines, rubber bands, and string. Enclose electrical wires in plastic tubing.

- Check your pet's collar each month. Make sure it isn't too tight. You should be able to fit two fingers underneath the collar. Snap on an ID tag and a license and you're all set for a stroll.

- Never leave your pet locked inside a car. Summer's heat will turn the car into an oven. Winter's chill will cause frostbite. Don't tie your pet up outside a store while you go inside, even for a second. He can be stolen in an instant.

- Remember to give your critter a daily dose of love, the best gift of all!